Charlie
the Spider
and Friends

A Spider Pac's Book

RON
&
JOANNE GALLO

SARA GALLO
Contributing Author/Editor

To order additional copies of this book, contact:
Xlibris
844-714-8691
www.Xlibris.com
Orders@Xlibris.com

ISBN: Softcover   978-1-6698-0432-1
        EBook   978-1-6698-0431-4

Print information available on the last page

Rev. date: 03/25/2022

Don't let schooling interfere with your education.

—Mark Twain

The most interesting information comes from children,
for they tell all they know and then stop.

—Mark Twain

Spider Children's Book
Spider Book: For children (ages 5–12)

CONTENTS

Patty the spider keeps coming back; she doesn't give up. You may knock her down but not out. She keeps coming at you.

Amber is always rebuilding, making adjustments when her home gets ruined. No matter the weather or war on her web, she moves forward.

Charlie is always content, no matter what flies into its web. It could be a beetle or a butterfly, no difference to him; he appreciates the blessing.

Sammy is a good steward of the things God has blessed her, not looking over her shoulder but using to the best of what God has blessed.

Follow Archie running through the grass taking care of the colony. Archie knows how to work as a team member. He and his friends are not anxious about anything and do not get stressed when something bad happens. They just work together to solve the problem as a team. This is called teamwork.

We are his child, children, childlike. No matter how old you are, you will always be his child. Once we understand this, then we see the world through a different lens, and our relationship to God is not in arrogance but in humbleness.

Thought for the day

The spider teaches us patience as well as perseverance. We need to be patient and wait on God in all things.

Preface

This gem of wisdom is not just for the child but for the parent. It first explores the world of the spider and the ant as Ranger Ron is walking through their playground. Each one of the smallest of God's creatures explains to Ranger Ron how God has instilled in each of his creature's characteristics that God wants his humans to see. God has picked the smallest to speak to the largest. God never mentions to "look at man" in Proverbs chapter 30; he picks the smallest, the most undesirable/ugliest, and weakest and tells man to looks at these creatures, "For they are wise." Do you see where God's priorities are?

As you walk with Ranger Ron through the garden, listen to the wisdom of each of God's creatures and from that you will gain an understanding of God's gems.

As a bonus, Ron provides more diamonds of wisdom and knowledge of a child, and by learning more about your child, you will be not only a better parent but have a better understanding of yourself in his kingdom.

Thought for today

I have been blessed with over forty years being a park ranger, to be able to see the spider and the ant as most people don't. God has shown me over the years in my daily walks through nature paths in the woods how fascinating not only nature is but also how he uses the least likely of creatures, and even people to show us his examples of his love and how he wants us to walk in the Christian life. Why doesn't God use the almighty, the powerful to give us the example? It's not how God operates; he always does the opposite of how man thinks and acts. God uses the poor, the lowly, the weak, misfits. I'm glad I'm one.

I hope you and your child enjoy this book as much as I enjoyed writing it. It was special to me. I would encourage you not to miss out on my other books, *Balance*, *When I Look Up*, and *The Spider and the Saint*. Learn more in detail about how God uses the spider and the ant to show us how to live the Christian life. Get more precious wisdom from *Balance*, a big book that each one is a gem that you will treasure forever and a book that you will pass on for future generations I believe. My book *When I Look Up* is another fantastic gem in learning about the child. For when you understand the child, you understand yourself. Do you want to know how the Lord wants you to be, look at a child. God uses a child as another example like the spider and the ant to display our Christian walk in life.

Proverbs 30:24–28.

The spider and the ant, "even though they are small, they are exceedingly wise" (v. 24).

PREFACE

All four of these spiders are my friends. Oh, I didn't introduce you to myself. I'm Park Ranger Ron Gallo. Well, you can call me Ranger Ron. In my many years in the outdoor field, I have observed spiders and ants and have found them fascinating. Over many years, I met several friends from the forest; four of these were spiders and an ant. Oh, you may not think to look at these creatures as anything special, most people don't. Well, that's unfortunate because God wants us to, and he says in Proverbs chapter 30 (in the Bible) we should look at these guys and learn from them. All of my friends have different strengths in their characteristics, but I will let each one describe to you each unique quality God has given them as a spider and an ant and to you as a person as well.

THANK YOU

I would like to thank my wife Joanne and Sara Gallo for there thoughts, wisdom and understanding that helped the book to become a success.

INTRODUCTION

This children's book will introduce the reader to four special spiders and one smart ant. All of them have the same characteristics, but each one will show how God uses this special quality in a spider's and an ant's life and will show how it can be applied in the child's daily walk with God and carry it in their future. God shows whether you work alone as the spider or with a team of ants the problem gets solved, and things get done through the faith and power that God gives us.

CHAPTER 1

Patty the Perseverant

*In the places I go there are things that I see that I
never could spell if I stopped with the Z.*

—Dr. Seuss

Patty the spider keeps coming back; she doesn't give up. You may knock her down but not out. She keeps coming at you.

Are you and your friends excited to go to the park today? Look! There is a man with a big smile and a funny hat is standing by the gates of the park. "Hi, I'm Ranger Ron. Let's take a walk through the woods, and see if we can find some of my friends. I think they are out doing their yard work right now." he says.

As you walk down the trail, you see the park is full of interesting plants and animals of all shapes, sizes, and colors. You come up to a big tree with twisted up roots and a delicate silvery web. Excitedly, Ranger Ron points at the web and says, "Oh, I see Patty on her web in the tree."

"Excuse me, Patty, I don't mean to bother you right now, but I see you're working on your web."

You hear a sweet tinkling voice say "Hello, Ranger Ron! Yes, I've been in such a rush to finish this web all day!" as a tiny spider slides gracefully down her silver thread.

"Well, Patty, I have some explorers here that would like to learn how a web is formed."

The tiny spider quickly glides to the edge of her web to peer down at you and your friends. "Hello explorers! You see, all spiders have silk glands that produce silk. We have several **spinnerets**. Think of these like tunnels that silk comes out of. We have several so we can decide which size silk we need for the part of the house—or web—we are making.

The thicker sections of silk will shoot out to create the outer section of my web. This is thicker because it needs to hold the web in place on trees, plants, bushes, and branches. It's the basic foundation of the web."

Then Patty runs to the middle of her web, dangling from the nearly invisible threads you realize you didn't even see a moment ago. "The inner silk section is my living room, kitchen, and bedroom. The silk here is a little thinner so I can move around easier. It's also harder for my meals to see."

"How do you keep from getting stuck in your own web?" asks Ranger Ron.

With a wiggle of her dainty legs, Patty explains "I also have oil glands on my feet, which allow me to move around the web without getting stuck in it like an insect would."

Suddenly a gust of wind blows some leaves right through Patty's beautiful web, tearing some of it down.

"Oh no!" cried Patty, "I worked all morning on this web." she said as she sadly bushed her leg against the torn strands.

Ranger Ron gently says, "Don't worry Patty. Just take a breath and remember that God designed you perfectly for fixing webs! Always remember what He says in Proverbs 46:10, 'to be still and know that I am God'. When you're still, God can help you see the best way to solve any problem. It's always better to be patient, and wait on God."

"You're right, Ranger Ron!" Patty squealed. "I just need to be still, (PATIENCE) and know that God is helping me to be the best web spinner I can be, even when wind and leaves come my way. I don't have to rush or leave. I can stand my ground, and never give up. I can rebuild after my web gets knocked over and down . . . do you ever have to try again?" When my web (Home) is broken, God has taught me to be patient. I don't move much, or at all, for I know that staying calm I can make a better decision on repairing any problems that occur. To get in a hurry and worried, makes anyone make bad decisions and needless worry over something that I know God is in control over anyway.

Ranger Ron chuckled and said, "Yes, Patty, we should always get back up and try again when obstacles knock us down. That is called **Perseverance**."

Patty smiled and said, "You know, boys and girls, God has given you a nature of perseverance just like we spiders have. It means to never give up. If you get knocked down, remember your spider friends and try again no matter what. Because you have the Lord in your heart, you can do anything!"

"That's right, Patty," said Ranger Ron. "Our good friend the apostle Paul said in Philippians 4:13, 'I can do all things through Christ who strengthens me.' King David, Moses, Abraham, and the apostle Paul are just a few people in the Bible who God called to persevere in doing what He had called them to do."

Patty took a deep breath and said, "Well, explorers, it was a pleasure meeting with you today, but I need to persevere through the problem and get started on rebuilding my web! Thank you for reminding me about God's blessing of **Perseverance and Patience**, Ranger Ron! Have a great day and keep on keeping on!" Thanks again Patty for showing us these great qualities we can learn from for our own life also.

Thought for Today:

Don't open the doors in life, let God do that, be patient and wait on him. If we do... we fall every time.

CHAPTER 2

Amber the Adjuster

I think I've discovered the secret of life—you just
hang around until you get used to it.

—Charles M. Schulz

Amber is always rebuilding, making adjustments when her home gets ruined.
No matter the weather or war on her web, she moves forward.

As we stroll through the garden, I see another one of my friends. It's Amber. "Hi, Amber, how are you doing?"

"I'm doing fine, Ranger Ron."

"Amber, I have my reader friends here, and I would like to know if you're not busy could you take a few minutes to tell our children about how a spider makes an *adjustment* during your daily life?"

"Well, Ranger Ron, I always have time for you. Well, boys and girls, you see a spider like all of us has to make adjustments. Things happen to us each day that we may not like. Things that are out of our control. But through prayer and walking with God, you can make those adjustments. Ron, I will give you one of many examples. One of my threads had gotten broken off and was blowing in the wind. I just made the adjustment and reattached that same thread that had broken off to another leaf or branch or twig. Ranger Ron, there is never a need to give up or get sad, just use the tools God has given you to redirect the adjustments to make it better."

"That is smart advice for our readers, Amber."

"So you see in my case when my web is broken or torn I don't run away and hide or pout or get sad. I just sit still for a few moments, then come back and rebuild the web, one silk strand at a time. Because of different circumstances, I may have to reset my silk strand at a different point on the tree limb. I may have to cut off or save old silk that was damaged. But either way, I adapt to new or different situations. Whether it's bad weather or something else disturbing my web, I will find a way to make the necessary adjustments to rebuild my web. My friend Patty shared with you about perseverance. Well, that's a part of it also. You need that as well while you're making the adjustments. God has instilled this in all of us spiders, but wait a moment, he has instilled it in you as well."

When you look at the Bible characters like Nehemiah, Joshua, Moses Gideon, and David, they all made adjustments to defeat their enemies.

"So whatever you go through in life, children, it's not that you will not encounter tough times. It's how you handle it that counts. Through God, you can find ways to adjust to any situation. Just have faith and he will show you new ways to handle any bad situation. God will make a way when there seems to be no way."

"Bye, Amber, see ya around."

"Bye, Ranger Ron."

Thought for today

When life gives you lemons, make lemonade. When God closes one door, he always opens another, even better.

Adjustment, children, means adapting or understanding a new situation and finding a way to overcome the situation.

CHAPTER 3

Charlie the Content

Charlie is always content, no matter what flies into its web. It could be a beetle or a butterfly, no difference to him. He appreciates the blessing.

As I walk down the path once again, I come upon another one of my friends. That is Charlie. "Hi, Charlie."

"Hi, Ranger Ron."

"Hey, Charlie, can you tell the kids about being content with what God has given you and why it's so important?"

"Sure. Ranger Ron. Well, boys and girls, you have seen my other friends so far Patty and Amber and Sammy and Archie will be right around the corner, and you will meet them too. Each one of those spiders including Archie the ant explains their important gift that God has given all of us. They're all equally important, and each one has a special quality that makes them a special gemstone that you as human folks can learn from us through God. Even though all of us possess the same skill in doing God's will, each one can provide their own specialty that they enjoy the most and love to talk about it."

"I enjoy talking about being content. Well, boys and girls, first of all, what does it mean to be content? Do you know the meaning? Well, the apostle Paul talks about it in the book of Philippians. It means to be satisfied with what God gives you."

"No matter the size or whatever it is, we are to be content, happy, or satisfied with whatever God provides us because that was his decision. You see it's easy to be happy when you get what you want, but the true test is to be happy or content no matter what God supplies because he knows better."

"Pertaining to myself as a spider, when an insect flies in my web, it doesn't matter if it's a bee or a butterfly, it's still a meal to me. It all tastes the same. So likewise when your parent gives you something, it can be a gift, a chore to do around the house, any other item, or just going out and just doing something with your dad and mom, be satisfied or content with whatever they give you or do for you. Remember it comes from their heart, and they're doing the best they can, and ultimately, boys and girls, it all comes from God."

"You see, my friends and I, including my friend the ant, we don't make a home, our spider web or ant mound, in one tree, plant, or anywhere and say, 'God, I wish I was over there about ten feet away from where there is better light and wind and more of a chance for the insects to fly into my web.' Where I place my web, from God's guidance, not my own, I will depend on God to supply. That, boys and girls, is called faith like you should have in your daily walk with God. God is not going to place me in a certain location to build my web and not supply me with the insects or with you anything else. The Bible says, 'Christ will supply all your needs in Christ Jesus.' So what's the theme or moral of this story about contentment? Don't worry about what's happening over there or with another person. Look at yourself. God will provide for you in his way and his timing."

"All he asked me to do is just be still. Psalm 46:10 says, 'Be still and know that I am God.' Be on my web and wait on God just like he wants you to do.

"Well, it was great meeting with you today. Say hi to my friend Sammy the Spider as you walk down the path. I think he is going to give you a lesson on being a good steward or manager. Goodbye for now, catch you on the next thread."

CHAPTER 4

Sammy the Good Steward

Sammy is a good steward of the things God has blessed her, not looking over her shoulder but using to the best of what God has blessed.

As Ranger Ron is walking through this garden forest, he spots an old friend Sammy the Spider. "Hi, Sammy.

"Hi, Ranger Ron."

"How are you doing today?"

"Well, Ranger Ron, I'm blessed. God has given me another leaf and even a straw this time to help me build my straw."

"You even got a straw. Also, Sammy . . ."

"Yes, Ranger Ron. Someone dropped a straw yesterday on the path and I am using it. I like to use all the things God has provided, even ones that don't come from trees."

"Sammy, can you tell my friends what you do with the straw and other items you find on the ground and on trees."

"Well, Ranger Ron, I would like your friends to know is that us spiders are good stewards of what the Lord has given us. This means that we use just about anything that we can help make our web stronger and helpful. We will not make a web on one plant or tree and worry about the tree across from us or whether there is enough sunlight or wind to bring over the insects as food. We are good stewards or managers of the web we're in. And we depend that God will supply us since he is the designer of the web we are in, not us."

"We pick up everything from paper, sticks, leaves, twigs, pieces of a cup, strings. When God sees that he can trust us with the simple, natural blessings like the leaves and the twigs that we are accustomed to seeing, he will provide for us other blessings not natural in the environment. But we have to be good stewards of the simple things he provides to us first, and he will see if he can trust us with the other blessings or favor."

"You and your friends have the same God, and he will do the same for you too."

"Well, Ranger Ron and your friends, it was nice speaking to you today. I hoped you learned something today about being a good steward. Before you go, Ranger Ron and boys and girls, take a look and look at your arms and legs. God gave them to you for a special purpose. Are you being *good stewards* of them when using them? Bye now, friends."

CHAPTER 5

Archie the Ant

Follow Archie running through the grass taking care of the colony. Archie knows how to work as a team member. He and his friends are not anxious for anything and do not stress when something bad happens. They just work together to solve the problem as a team. This is called teamwork.

As Ranger Ron is walking through the grass almost getting to his home, he spots Archie. "Hey, Archie!"

"Hi, Ranger Ron."

"It is so nice to see you today. I hope I'm not keeping you from anything."

"No, you're never a bother, Ranger Ron."

"Archie, I have my friends with me today, and I was wondering if you can tell them some great things that you do as ants that are so wonderful."

"Well, Ranger Ron, I would like to tell the boys and girls this, that first of all, ants work in teams, teamwork. We believe there is no *I* in a team. When we need to get a job done like moving a pebble from the ant mound opening or building the mound. We do it together, not alone. Also, we have roles or assigned jobs. The worker ants don't try and be the queen, and the queen doesn't try to be the search ant. When something bad happens like a small stone gets put over our opening in our home mound, we don't panic. We just either move it away or just tunnel to another spot."

"So whenever you have a problem, seek out other people to help you. Even if they are all different and working in different areas, you must learn you cannot do it many times on your own."

"Well, boys and girls, that's all the time we have for today. It was a great walk through the garden. I hope that maybe one day we can join together for another walk down spider land. God bless you."

Thoughts for Today:

1. An ant and an earth worm can turn up (plow) an acre of land in a day, more than a plow/tractor.

2. Many times God will turn a leaf over just before it rains, so the underside (dull side) is out so it can get wet. God wants both sides of the leaf to be shiny... to show off its beauty, that He has created...

3. Ranger Ron has seen spiders pick up more than 100- 500x their weight...

Chapter 6

After the Storm

The next day, a big storm ran in our area, and it rained all day and into the night. The garden and forest had gotten a lot of rain and wind. Some trees were knocked down. The following day after, the sun came back out, and I was excited to get back into the garden where my friends were to see how they were doing. Before I walked outside, I saw on the news where folks were upset and arguing back and forth over matters in our country.

My children looked at me and asked, "Dad, why cannot they agree with each other?"

I explained to them, "Kids, man has a pride problem, but as you see in nature whether it be with animals, insects, our human body, or the solar system, they all *understand* the role they have on earth. Man because of his free will doesn't and wants to naturally go against the things of God by nature."

I took them out to the garden to show them my friends. As we walked together, what do you think we saw? After the storm, we saw all my friends doing what they do best, using God's gifts to the best and for him. There was no bickering, arguing, conducting a board meeting. No, each one in their own web was doing what God instilled them to do. There we saw Patty not worried that her web was destroyed by the rain or wind storm. She just used perseverance and made the repairs and she spun around. Amber was making adjustments and creating the web this time in a different design, using different twigs, branches, leaves to help build it after the web threads were broken off. She didn't give up. As I walked down the path, I noticed Charlie just sitting there with the wind still blowing a bit after the storm, just being content. He was not upset about the storm but survived. I looked up and noticed my other friend Sammy being again a good steward. He was bringing a straw and a piece of paper he found along with a small twig to help rebuild the web. Sammy knew that being a good steward, making the most of what God had given him was of greater importance, do we?

Before we walked off the path, we looked down, and I said, "Look, guys, there is Archie my friend the ant."
As Archie walked by with his twig, he looked up and said, "Hi, Ranger Ron."

I said hi back. I asked Archie, "How was it going?" He said, "Don't have time to talk this time, Ranger Ron. Sorry, too busy rebuilding our ant mound with my buddies. We all work as a team and had to make the adjustments like our friend the spider who lives above, and we created a new mound in a different location. Ranger Ron, by working as a team and not giving up is the key."

We all went back inside the house, and the kids said, "Dad, we learned something in our walk today."

I asked, "What was that, guys?"

They said, "Dad we learned that each one of those small creatures knew what to do even through the storm."
I said, "God has instilled the same in you. They put their trust in God. You can too!"

"Thanks, we love you."

"Love you too, kiddo."

Thought for today

"I have never driven through in a storm, that I never drove out of" (T. D. Jakes).

CHAPTER 7

Childlike:
For Parents and Kids

Children: Six points that we need to look at children to see ourselves through them. We take care of them when they are young, then they take care of us when we are old. It goes full circle.

1. He made children so we can emulate them into adulthood learning from obedience as a child. God didn't ask Adam and Eve to do push-ups and run laps through the forest. He said, "Don't eat from a certain tree." Obedience, learning that as a child will last us through adulthood.

2. Children are always looking up. Why do we stop? My encouragement, stop looking straight ahead at people. They can disappoint you whether it's world politics or your own circle

3. Children are innocent/humble. Why do we stop?

4. Be childlike, not childish. A child is trusting. Remember when you were growing up? Even though you didn't understand the mysteries of your world, you *trusted* that big person. Why does that stop?

5. Many times where the child is in the back car seat trying to tell Mom or Dad how to drive, we do the same thing to God. God is looking back and saying, "Would you shut up and let me drive?" LOL. We trust the inside of our body, oxygen, heartbeat, liver, brain, kidney function, the hard-wiring blood flow all on the inside, so how come we don't trust things on the outside? It's the same for God. It's called pride. It doesn't take pride in the big things. We take them for granted like the sun rising or setting, but when it comes to ourselves, we want to put God in a box and control him as we see fit in our lives. Try telling your employer when you're coming into work. Your professor when you feel like taking that test, you fail to take the doctor's prescription to get better. So why do we follow man's rules, but when it comes to God's, we are the only one who opens or closes our eyes.

6. Children are trusting. Why do we stop? Remember when you were growing up, you always *trusted* in that *big* person, your parents, grandparents, aunt, uncle, teacher. Why does that stop? Remember we are his children. It doesn't matter if you're 1,000 years old.

You will always be his child. A parent doesn't want a child to look at another child for guidance and direction, so why do we look at people? They don't open your eyes in the morning, do they?

Thought for today

It was no coincidence that the Lord made children before he made adults. It's so we can see who he sees, childlike, not childish.

Do you know how God sees us? It's not how society looks at others with arrogance (I'm better than you, I have a degree or have awards, etc.). No, my friend, God sees all of us as just *tall children*.

CHAPTER 8

From a Teachers Perspective: Tips for the Parents

This is from Joanne Gallo, MS in elementary education with over thirty-three years experience as an elementary school teacher.

1. Be consistent in all that you do with your child.

2. Don't make promises to your kids that you cannot keep or might not be able to. Try using the word *maybe*, then you're not committing while also teaching about life. There is not always a guarantee.

3. Show an interest in everything your child tells you. It is very important to them.

4. If you do and get one thing for your child, do it for the rest.

5. The greatest thing you can give your child is not material things but *your time*. In my husband Ron's fishing booklet entitled *150 Fishing Tips for Your Child*, he advises, "When you take your child fishing, leave your fishing pole at home." It becomes too tempting for the parent to want to fish and not pay attention to their child when they need to. He also says, "Take a bucket and a field guide to aquatic nature." You can also step away from the fishing pole for a few minutes and catch minnows while teaching them about nature. Now this brings in *the full circle* for their love of nature.

6. Give your child a five-minute warning whenever you're going or leaving someplace. It helps to prevent tantrums about leaving or going.

7. Teach your child to help someone who needs help.

8. Teach your child to be thankful, and show it.

9. Teach your child to admit when he/she is wrong and to apologize if they made a mistake.

10. Teach your child not to be afraid to ask questions if they don't understand something or ask for help when they are in need.

11. Teach your child to stand up for what is right when they see something wrong.

12. Teach your child to say I love you to someone they love.

13. Teach them to love another even if that person *hurt* them as Jesus loves us.

14. Parents, remember you should be your child's greatest *role model*. You cannot say one thing and do another; they will see that.

15. Teach your child to pray in detail to God.

16. Teach your child the importance of spending time with God by reading the Bible or by having devotions.

17. Teach your child how much God loves him/her. When was the last time you gave your child a hug? I feel God hugging me every minute, just thinking about him.

18. Have your child put some money in an envelope for a tithe each week even if it's fifty cents from a chore done at home. At an early age, have them take out the money to pay the cashier at the store, not you. This teaches them about money and giving.

19. Have certain *standard templates* around the house for things they do around the house and not give them chore money for this. This teaches them about basic responsibilities. Anything above that, you can give them a little spending money when the work is completed.

20. When disciplining your child after sending them to the bedroom, go in and make them understand what they did and why it was wrong. Then the last thing you do is hug them. This ending leaves them on a positive note, instead of just leaving them in there.

21. Just look and listen to them. Men want to solve things quickly while women want you to just *listen* many times.

22. Ask your child to reflect for two minutes (you do it too) on the beauty of God and what he means to you.

23. When we used to take long trips, our kids would say (like many use this standard line).

24. You cannot have two chiefs in a family. The Bible says the husband should be the head of the household. But with this comes responsibilities and humbleness. If the wife is in control, the child will likely lose respect for the dad. If a dad makes a mistake (which will happen), the wife or child shouldn't say, "I told you so." Give him that reassurance and move on from it. Give him the support he needs. He already feels bad. Husbands listen to their wives and children in certain instances. It makes them feel needed, and part of the game loop, but you have to make the final decision in big situations. Being smart without strategies is useless. Generals get input from many even from the lower command.

25. Teach your child about money, management, and respect for others. The book of Proverbs gives gems you can teach children about God's principles in life.

Books by Ron Gallo

1. ***Balance***: (a three-volume set) Gems that will enrich your life. You will laugh, you will cry, and you will understand. Did you know that God points out the smallest and the world's most hideous creatures and tells man to look at them for wisdom? He never mentions to look at man. See where God's priorities are.

    Volume 1 *The Awakening*
    Volume 2 *The Spider, the Ant, and More Answers*
    Volume 3 *Treasury of More Gems*

2. ***Charlie the Spider and Friends***: (Children's book) Walk with Ranger Ron through the garden and see his spider friends and what they can teach you.

3. ***When I Look Up***: Learn about the child first, then we can understand the adult. Many of our books and sermons are focused on the *adult* side of how we should be. Unless you *understand* where you started, you cannot understand yourself and where and what God expects from us in his mission.

4. ***The Spider and the Saint***: Enrich yourself through various gems of knowledge and understanding. Learn how the spider teaches the saint about life.

Thought for today

Proverbs chapter 30 says the spider is small but wise. (Our children are small, and we as adults while there learning from us,) we're learning from them. They're wise as well.

Printed in the United States
by Baker & Taylor Publisher Services